ANGELS AND PATHWAYS

REBECCA J. STEIGER

Copyright 2025 by Rebecca J. Steiger

All rights reserved. This book or any portion thereof may not be reproduced or used in any manner whatsoever without the express written permission of the publisher except for the use of brief quotation in a book review.

ISBN 978-1-971940-31-1 (Paperback)
ISBN 978-1-971940-32-8 (Ebook)

Inquiries and Book Orders
should be addressed to:

Leavitt Peak Press
17901 Pioneer Blvd Ste L #298,
Artesia, California 90701
Phone #: 2092191548

Contents

Acknowledgments

As I dive into this book, digging deeper into your divine spiritual journey on self-discovery, I want to thank all the listeners on my talk shows and all my TikTok followers, my wonderful family and loved ones, friends, and especially all my clients. They not only validate my work but also keep me humble.

Introduction

I am an ordinary woman with extraordinary gifts given by God. I am an angelic channeler, and I see things others do not. I am the receiver of messages from the angels who are God's messengers.

Imagine looking out your front door and seeing volcanoes erupting, earthquakes, tornadoes. Mountains will crumble, and all the seas, oceans, and some of rivers will catch fire. *It will happen.* Why? The earth is so polluted by man it has to burp it all out and cleanse the earth. The earth is like a human stomach; if you eat food that causes food poisoning, you are going to get sick, throw up, have diarrhea, even risk dying—unless you take medication and the toxins leave your system.

The earth is the same way. Man has dumped so much waste into Mother Earth that it has literally made the earth sick. We have done the same thing to our seas and oceans. Volcanoes will erupt beneath the water, causing a spark to ignite all the gas and oil lines that run under the seas and oceans. You say that cannot be done. Never limit the power of Mother Earth and God.

We have created a horrible situation—all in the name of greed. The tsunamis will take the coastlines back. Open your eyes and look around you. Look at all the trash and the debris around you; 90 percent of that is going into the ground, in our oceans and seas or rivers, so this earth will be cleansed. We can either watch it unfold—or we can start healing this earth by doing our part to clean up the trash and debris, sending healing energy into the earth and universe.

You have to change your mindset and discover yourself before you can help with the healing. This book will help lead you to a new and wonderful path in your life—the next chapter of your life.

1

WHO IS REBECCA J. STEIGER?

I am an ordinary person who has extraordinary gifts given to me by God! I am an angelic channeler. I see things others don't. I see angels. I receive messages from the angels—God's messengers. I write and speak through the angelic realm after I had a near-death experience and stood before God, who sent me back to do his work in a loving and positive way. I found my mission, my purpose, my passion—helping others in a loving and positive way.

Imagine looking out your front door and seeing volcanoes erupting, earthquakes and all the seas, oceans, and lots of large rivers on fire. It will happen. Why? The earth is so polluted by man it has to burp it all out to cleanse itself. The earth is like a human's stomach; if you eat bad food that causes food poisoning, you are going to get sick and throw up, have diarrhea. In the same way, the earth reacts to toxins. Man has dumped so much waste into Mother Earth that it has literally made the earth sick and threw it off its axis.

We have also done the same thing to our seas and oceans. Volcanoes erupt under them, causing a spark to ignite all the gas and oil lines beneath the seas and oceans. We have created the tsunamis that will take back the coastlines. Open your eyes, and look at all the trash and debris around you. Ninety percent of that is going into the ground and the oceans—all in the name of progress.

The universe is experiencing the same thing. We are polluting it as well with obsolete satellites that are floating around with no direction and have been left there until some of them disintegrate. We are exploring the other worlds, looking for life on other planets, when we know there are frequent claims of UFOs flying around this earth all the time. So why are we looking in space? When are we going to open our eyes to what is happening? Are we going to wait until the grids go down from sun flares? If we do, we will be going back to the old ways—no electricity, cars won't start, food supply will disappear, no cell phones, and life will change. Are you ready?

These are the things that I see. I love what I do. I am who I am, and I wrote this book for you—so you can find your divine mission and spiritual mission in this life.

Metaphysical moment:

Life is a boneyard of simple mistakes.

2

When a Bright Sunny Day Holds Tragedy in the Night

It was a perfect spring day in April 1993—sunshine, blue skies, seventy-five degrees, not a cloud in sight.

I went to the barn to ride and train horses, enjoying working and watching the horses work up a slight sweat. I knew they had reached their peak for the day, so I cooled them out then put them back in their stalls.

My four-year-old grandson was coming to visit, and that was always fun. When he got there, as usual, he was full of energy; and as we played, he wanted to dig fishing worms. Well, the best place for that was behind the barn, where the dirt was the richest. We went and found an old coffee can in the tack room, got a scoop shovel, and we were off to a new adventure, digging worms. Our digging was successful, providing us with enough worms that we could go fishing in the neighboring pond in the morning.

As twilight came, we decided to go to the mobile home we were living in until our new house was finished. Thank goodness we will be moving next week. Little boys love hot dogs, mac and cheese, so we feasted on that. I was really tired; it had been a long day, and we both were dirty. Next was bathtime. After we had both bathed and got our PJs on, we sat down to watch TV.

Suddenly it started storming, with rain pounding on the roof. The weather forecast came on the TV and said "storms only," so no need to worry. Then my grandson said, "Beck, let's go to bed." I agreed, and so we went to the back bedroom, where the water-bed was; he liked to sleep on that. We had just said his prayers.

Hearing a large clap of thunder, he said, "I'm scared."

The thunder was really rolling. I told him it was okay, that it was just a storm. About that time, it sounded like a bomb went off, and I told him to jump on my chest and put his arms around me, and I rolled over to protect him. He did, and everything went dark—a darkness like you have never seen or felt, like falling into a black hole. I kept telling him to hold on, just keep holding on; it will be over in a minute. I felt something hit me in the head and thought that it must be the washing machine.

The next thing I knew, I was standing in a dark room, in a shaft of light. I was no larger than a head of a straight pin. I was looking at a huge sandstone desk where the outline of God was. The light was behind God, who was holding a quill pen in his hand, and the book of life was on his desk. I felt profound love and peace as I stood there.

God turned the page in the book of life and said, "On November 3rd you did…"

At that instant, my sister-in-law, Diane, who had died a year and a half ago came in. She was wearing an all-white dress and walked around God and tapped him on the shoulder and said, "Not now, Lord, for she has many things to do."

It took me a long time to realize that I was in God's room—not the light but in God's room. At that instant, I woke up outside under a satellite dish that looked like a wilted flower in the yard, about seventy feet behind the mobile home. My grandson was right beside me. I sat up and urged him to wake up. When he didn't immediately respond, I started to panic. I reached over and shook him, and he then woke up and sat up and said to me, "I'm wet and cold. Let's go somewhere."

I didn't know that the house was gone as well as the mobile home—blown away.

Little did I know there were live power lines all around us. I got up and picked him up and looked around and thought, *If there is hell, this must be what it looks like.*

I looked at the barn, and it looked okay. The horse trailer looked okay. Little did I know that the trailer was sitting in the alleyway of the barn, and everything behind that had collapsed, trapping the horses in their stalls. So I walked over five acres of debris that I never saw and did not get one cut; and as I went to cross the creek that ran though the pasture, I was thinking that I had heard that tornadoes can wash up snakes, so how was I going to cross with my grandson in my arms?

Then a shaft of light showed on a flat rock in the creek, and I stepped on the rock and crossed the creek. We should not have survived, yet we did. We should have died, yet we were saved.

Everything in your life can change in the blink of an eye—and that is how my spiritual journey and divine mission began.

Metaphysical moment:

See the beauty in all things!

3

Rainbows

Out of the storm comes a bright and beautiful rainbow lighting up the sky with a spectrum of color, leading to the end, where we wish for a pot of gold. Look closely, and you can see the creation of God. Look even closer, and you can may glimpse the angels that watch over us constantly, connecting us to earth and also to the Spirit—the Supreme Being, the healer of all, the creator of all. Follow me, and learn about the angels, the messengers of God, who help us in all things that we do.

Learn how to accomplish tranquility and peace through divine love, how to trust in yourself by opening yourself to the angelic realm of possibilities! Feel the freedom, love, and deep devotion you will receive from the angels.

So get ready to embark on the greatest, most fulfilling journey of your life, leaving darkness to stand and rejoice in the love and light that the Spirit and the angels provide for you, making you whole and complete in body, mind, and spirit.

What is the secret? There isn't one—only love and understanding of what is happening within and around you, what a beautiful and profoundly powerful person you can become because you already are; you just don't know it.

Looking in a mirror can be terrifying or beautiful, a sight to behold. It can reflect love, light, tranquility, and peace.

Won't you change your word from strife and disappointment to living life to the fullest? I will show you how to let go of the past—the anger toward life that you carry like a badge of honor, the sorrows you feel for yourself and your life. I will help lift you higher than you have ever imagined!

Metaphysical moment:

How do you want to live your life?

4

WHAT IS LIFE?

This is a chapter that I could make a book out of. Life is a tangle of knowledge, love, and regret, repeating mistakes, learning valuable lessons, and receiving precious gifts. However, in this chapter, I am only giving you the basics of what life is about and how to change the negative into positive.

What is life all about? Why does life give us so many trials and tribulations? Is life just an illusion or an experience? So many questions still left unanswered.

Think about all that we, as humans, have experienced in life. Not all of it is bad, hurtful, or depressing. Jobs change, partners change—or we have no partners because we cannot find the right one. We look; we try everything from going out to dating sites to finding someone on social media. Then when we do, we still lose what we have worked so hard to find. Sometimes there are small children involved—then we both become parents. Then we have to find the strength to carry on and still have time to not only love our children, but also teach them how to become loving and caring adults. Then we finish our jobs and send them out into the world to find their own way.

Being a parent, however, is never going to end. No matter how old our children are, they still need their parents, their family. As we grow older, we hope to be wiser, then we are slapped in the face with another problem or ten other problems. However, God never gives us more than we can handle. Faith is our rock! From every problem we have, we gain two things—knowledge and strength. We become stronger from the problems we have to face and deal with. Sometimes it's a test of faith.

Sometimes we feel the weight of the world on our shoulders. We still feel alone, but being alone is only an illusion. We are never alone; your angels are always with you, waiting for you to ask them for what you want or need. When you learn how to use your angels to help you, life becomes easier. Everything works for you in divine timing. We need to just let it go and allow the angels and the universe to take care of our problems. You need to feel the divine love the angels provide for you. So many people are sceptics when it comes to believing in the angelic realm. They don't think they are with them, they don't think they can use them, and they sure don't think you can see them. Well, guess what—all things are possible in this life when you wake up and try using them or talking to them.

I personally see angels; I personally use my angels for everyday living. They are with everyone. You are born with a guardian angel to help you though this life. They do everything for you. They create miracles for you. They protect you from harm, yet do you think these things happen without their divine love? No, you do not. Look around you and see all creation—the plants, the grass, your children—are all miracles. You are a miracle! You are God's greatest masterpiece. You were created by God's divine love. God never gives us more than we can handle, so handle your life in a more positive way through the use of your angels. We learn from our mistakes and then we receive our gift or gifts. We never stop learning or receiving gifts in this life. It helps us to continue to grow mentally. It helps us to overcome obstacles. So do not let yourself down by refusing your angels, a gift to you from our creator.

When we are presented with a problem, we need a solution. We need it to end in a positive way. By letting go of negativity, a new solution will quickly come. By flipping the coin from negative to positive, we can charge and change the outcome of the problem. I know sometimes this is hard. However, sometimes life is hard. Even beautiful things, like a rose, have thorns, don't they? So we have to handle them with care, or else that thorn will prick our skin, causing pain. Save yourself from the pain of the problem by handling the problem through love and care of the angels. When we do this, we will then have time to experience joy, peace and tranquility. We find self-love. That, my friends, is the greatest thing we can accomplish in this life.

Metaphysical moment:

Who is guiding your life?

5

LIVING IN THE SPIRIT

Living in the Spirit means just that—truly living in the Spirit.

If the Spirit heard every thought you ever had, every word you ever spoke, what would you do differently? Guess what—he does. Now what if God thought those thoughts and words were prayer? What would you do differently? Would you speak differently?

We all see things differently; we all think differently.

The one thing that you know best in this world is yourself. You know things about yourself and your thoughts better than anyone else does. Everything that you think you have hidden within yourself is not so, for the Spirit and the angelic realm know. You cannot hide even your deepest secrets, wishes, fears from them. However, they are great secret keepers. Do not worry—you are not being judged.

Learn to focus inside yourself—how you feel, how you think, and what you speak!

A loving Supreme Being surrounds us all! Through his love, we are nurtured, grow, and live. We are here on this heavenly earth to learn the lessons, receive the gifts, and play. Play is very important, for when we play, we forget the daily stress, all of life's pressure. Even as adults, we need to enjoy life and let our inner child come out to play. We need to dance and touch the earth. You need to find out who you are—truly are—and why you are here. Let me tell you, you are here to grow and connect—mentally, spiritually, and physically.

God gives you the freedom of choice, the power of thought that comes from the mind. Let us all be individuals. This gives you the power to change your lives, your minds, and your thoughts.

He is the Supreme Master of art, for he made us all—this earth, the creatures upon it, and the heavenly stars above. Look around you and see; feel the life that surrounds you—the beauty, the peace.

Some say we should fear God our creator. How can you fear such a loving entity—the Creator of all!

No matter what happens to you in this life, you must always have strength and determination.

6

WHAT STONES PROVIDE

Nature provides us with many gifts—one being the history and stories of the stone. Some stones are very healing—very powerful, full of energy from the earth. They can be either healing and beautiful, like a quartz crystal, amethyst, or many other healing stones. Some can be deadly such as a boulder that can crush you.

All these stones have natural iron and minerals contained within them.

My personal stones come from the sacred ground where I live. These stones may have formed and came from the caves that surround me, hidden from the view until now. They may have come from ancient burial grounds that are here on this land.

They may have come from my natural spring. Each stone is handpicked by me to ensure it holds the highest vibrational energy and quality.

These stones I have blessed with health, spiritual guidance, and calming energy. Each stone is unique, and no stones are ever alike.

When you are hunting the stone for you, place the stone that catches your eye, put it in the palm of your left hand, and see if the energy is working for you. When you hold the stone, it will share its story—how it was formed, where it came from. Does it give you comfort and energy? What do you get from a stone?

Remember, all things upon this earth have life, have a story to tell us in their own way. One of the biggest history lessons we will ever receive is from stones. It could be a fossil, a drusy, or even contain gold. However, stones are better than money. They tell us the history of our ancestors' lives, our lives, the very beginnings of the land itself.

I am a history buff, curious about my ancestry and how my family lived a hundred years ago. The stones give us so much insight into these—the tools they made out of stone, the cookware they used, the fires they cooked on and stayed warm with.

Do we not build our lives on stepping stones, helping us to advance farther in our faith and become who God intended us to be? Do we not cling to the rock of life, not letting go, to move forward in life, clinging to the rock out of fear of change? It is always in our best interest and outcome to face the unknown of a new and different way of life. That can be so beautiful and wonderful. All you have to do is let go of the rock and believe in God and the angels. Then you will learn how to truly be moving forward in your life—happy, healthy feeling loved.

We also throw stones at others in this life, which means talking about others when they are down or moving away from someone or a situation. Stones can be beautiful or so hurtful. We should never throw stones. Instead of throwing stones, we need to have compassion for that person.

We are here to help others in their time of need. We need to help others in a positive way and not kick them when they are down. You never know—you might be the next one who is down.

We threw stones in ancient wars. David slayed Goliath with a slingshot, using a single stone. Stones can be beautiful or deadly, depending on how you choose to use them.

No matter how we live, stones are an important part of our lives. They are the foundations that your life is built on.

Metaphysical moment:

Everything you see and touch has its own energy!

7

EVERYTHING HAS A LIFE OF ITS OWN

Everything has a life of its own—the trees, flowers, grass, birds, animals, even wool from a sheep. All is here now and in the wintertime of life, but they seem to die or disappear, arriving again after the long days of winter— or simply not blooming or coming alive. Why? Because the cycle of life never ends. There is a time to live, a time to die, and a time for new growth—the life cycle.

We all see winter as a time for dark days and dying. However, when children laugh, our hearts fill with joy, and we can't help but smile. Snow helps clean the air and makes a wonderland, lighting the trees and ground with a million light diamonds—perfect, peaceful, and beautiful. A rose can bloom in the snow, and a bird will sing despite the cold. Therefore, the darkness is gone, replaced by the joy of others—those that stay dormant and rest to rejoice in the spring, blooming more beautiful when the soft rain and sunshine bring them back to life.

There is a time when all of nature is busy, enjoying the spring. Tender leaves peep through, reaching carefully toward the light, feeling the warmth. Life begins again for all things young and tender, always grounded, reaching and stretching for the light of growth, enjoying the drink God provides by the gentle rain that occasionally falls.

By summer, the hearty leaves now bloom and are strong, blooming and providing nourishment to others. Birds and bees suck the nectar of life, and in return, they grow stronger and help spread the seed of life somewhere else.

Hot lazy days, lemonade, and barbeques, enjoying our families and neighbors—fall sweeps away the life of summer, turning green leaves into beautiful colors falling to the earth to cover the blooms of life for a little longer until spring arrives again. The skies turn gray, and the wind blows. Again, there is winter.

Our lives turn in cycles just like the earth cycles.

We are born to enjoy the sun and sleep in the darkness. How has that changed as we grow older? So many people are still asleep, never having felt the light, always in the darkness. They have stayed asleep in their minds and hearts, never reaching, never experiencing the light. Why? Because they cannot see—they truly cannot see—and they have no idea to really feel joy or love. Therefore, they wither and die—leaving what behind? Constant fear, to have never enjoyed life.

Life is a precious gift given to us by God—to spread our wings in flight and feel the sun in our lives, to enjoy the gentle cleansing of the rain, and to give ourselves permission to laugh, love, and hope, to feel good instead of bad, to sing when we want and to play when we want.

Through lessons we receive gifts, we receive knowledge, sharing the knowledge with others so they too can receive the gift. Therefore, they can pass it on.

Letting go—truly letting go—of the pain of the past is the hardest thing one will do because this pain is familiar to us; it is like a blanket of protection, keeps us from getting involved. With who? Yourself, of course. It keeps you in social acceptance because everyone you know is in some sort of pain—depression, physical illness—things that all your friends and family expect to talk about, to dream about.

Life can be so much more exciting and fulfilling. Life can open a beautiful rose for you, creating memories of joy, peace, love, and laughter by opening your heart and mind; by using your light to surround you and go in front of you; by trusting yourself in the goodness of God and loving God; by using your gardening tools to pull the weeds out of your life, your mind, your body; by freeing yourself from others and listening to your "God self."

Free yourself. Free your family and friends. Stand in the light of love and healing. Learn that all is not as it may seem, that God does have a plan for you and your life—a perfect plan showing you that you too can grow from the light like all of God's creatures—

freeing you from illness and strife, letting you laugh, love, and experience living.

Learning is a natural process. We never quit learning, never quit using our mind. When we quit using our mind, we shut ourselves off; we no longer exist, we can no longer survive in the world, and we are buried deep under the blanket of snow. Our thinking process is what keeps us going—sometimes in the wrong direction. Sometimes you are trapped. By melting away the snow, you become able to see more clearly and are able to redirect your mind, creating a clearer view of your life. Then the sun appears. The light shines on your path, showing you all things are possible, freeing you to stand solid and walk the path God has planned for you. In doing so, your heart will bloom and open to let you see—to truly see not only life, but also to view others differently.

By doing so, you become a beautiful garden of many colors. Your beauty will shine brightly. Your inner beauty will become outer beauty. When you give and share your new-found knowledge in a loving, positive way, others will seek to follow you, then their minds and hearts can be used to fulfill their God-given destiny.

We are all different, yet we are all the same. Why? Because we all have the same creator—God! We are simply different human forms, following different teachings from family and life experiences. Some teachings are good and positive; some are misguiding, even brutal. If you use your mind, you can change the brutal acts into positive learning lessons. Changing the mind is not always a bad thing, and you become a positive person, a more giving, sharing, loving person.

Given time, your opinion will change because you have changed. You will bend with the breezes of life. By bending, you will strengthen your mind and heart, nourishing your body and mind like a cool drink of water on a sunny day. You will grow stronger, and the sun will nourish you. Sorrow and grief will disappear.

Anger is the one thing that keeps most people going. Anger creates nothing, but it fuels most people. It also creates illness of the body and mind. If you take away nothing else from this book, let it be this: Anger is consuming the minds and hearts of those who refuse to open themselves to see. Change your opinion of yourself first and then others. Tear down the wall of negativity, and replace those thoughts of anger, greed, and jealousy with thoughts of healing, love, and positive opinion of what is taking place around you. Show your emotions; feel your emotions for yourself and others.

Do not tread on the earth, but help protect it. Help protect the good of the earth and universe. Help protect your neighbor by giving yourself; you are receiving a wonderful gift of love when you do. You are learning that to give, you also receive so much more; but first, you have to open the door of your house, clean out all the dirt, even in the corners, and stand solid on the earth. This will allow you to reach greater heights in your life, allowing you to soar with the eagles, and all this can be done simply by opening one door—the mind. Use it wisely.

We are not meant to lead a solitary existence but to share our lives, our knowledge, with others. We are to learn and teach, and in doing so, we live. What good is it if you know all the wonderful things and keep them locked away in your mind? How can others learn if you will not share your knowledge? Don't think you don't have anything to give or share; we all have something we can share with others. It may not be an important thing to you, but it may be a wonderful thing to someone else.

Not all in life is good. True, but we can make things better by learning to cope, by realizing that life has many lessons and beyond today is tomorrow, where you can see things more clearly. Others have taught you to listen to them, do what they say, what they tell you to do. Now I say through God—listen to yourself and God. You are an individual, the creator of your own world. Take the power you were given and use it. Do not turn the power you were given over to another person. It is giving away your life, your control! So take your power back; listen to God and self.

Take responsibility for your actions, your life. If you do not like something, say so. If you like something, say so. All you have to do is use your power to live your life. You will immediately feel stronger when you reclaim your power, your knowledge, and your life. Do not shut others out, but draw them into your life with your power of knowledge. Receive them graciously. Hold you head high, and walk with straightness, squaring your shoulders in power, not slumped in anger or sorrow. Let your burdens go, lifting you higher in this realm. See yourself and all things differently. You will no longer exist, but you will be living. What a wonderful gift.

We all have choices—choose yours carefully. Redirect your energies. Feel! Think! By doing the above, you will not only feel better, but also look better. Remember, only you, not another man, can make the choices that are best for you. Remember that not everyone is on your path, that others have issues, and their path may not coincide with yours.

Give others space so that they learn and see their own way. Do not try to force them. The choice is theirs; the work is theirs. Just because you share your life with someone does not mean they are on the same path as you. We are all individuals, and our thoughts are our own. Let them walk their path, lending a helping hand when they need it, but let them find their own way. Do not worry; they will eventually get it—or not. Your purpose is to remain aware of what's happening around you. Be your own keeper of the light. They have to have their own experiences in life apart from yours. What they see may be different—not wrong, simply different.

If five people witness the same accident, there will be five different versions of how it happened. Every one of us sees things a little differently, but all five people helped make the story complete. What good is knowledge if you do not share it in your own way? It may be seen differently than someone else's experience though the information is the same.

Be the powerful person you were meant to be—a unique individual shaped by the hands of God!

Metaphysical moment:

Thank you, Lord, for
the blessings we take for
granted every day.

8

PATIENCE

Are you an impatient person? Do you want it done now? Most of us are! They say patience is a virtue. Is it, or does it create laziness? What happens when you ask for patience? Patience will try you! That is why I never ask for patience.

Instead of asking for patience, I have found what really works for me—I ask, "Does it belong on my path? Is this for me?" Because not everything has a purpose for you—it may be meant for the person next to you. However, we are all on different paths in this life. What belongs to one does not belong on another.

I believe that we should ask for guidance, direction, and knowledge. We need to turn patience into direction—show me the path I need to take to make this happen. Lead with love and direction. Your path must align with your purpose to bring this to life. Some words are instantly calming, but the word *patience* frustrates us right away. When we are resistant, we get stuck on our path. Creating resistance is like pulling too hard on a closed door—nothing happens. We are just wasting our energy. Knowing the right way to open it unlocks the door to all things. You can have patience, wait for the door to open, and eventually someone will open it for you—if you are willing to sit there, depending on someone to come along, which could take a very long time.

Be aware of what you are doing and saying. Be aware of the energy that surrounds you when you are asking for directions. If it doesn't feel right, go to where the energy feels great because we are all individuals and everyone's energy is their own, some bad and some great, and there are some who have no energy—absolutely none. Do not give them yours; they will suck the life out of you. So instead, ask if this is the direction you need to go. Ask your angels for everything including directions.

So instead of asking for patience, ask for directions and guidance. Then the angels will give you both, making your life and your path easier and more fulfilling.

God is the ultimate
Judge—not you.

9

SELF-JUDGMENTS

Doubt, fear, failure, self-worth—do these things rule your life? Do you think you are not worthy to have the things others have? Do you feel like your life is going nowhere? That you are afraid to take a step outside the little square box you are in? Are you afraid you will fail at life if you take that one step? Do you not feel like you are good enough or look as good as your friends, neighbors, or the model in the magazine?

Do you ever challenge yourself and question yourself and your choices all the time? Do you feel incomplete and restless? Self-judgment creates doubts! It is a life killer, causing you to not live your life the way you want or see it.

You deserve to be happy in this life. You deserve to have what you want in this life. You deserve to believe in yourself. It is never too late to turn your life over to the Spirit and the angels and watch how quickly your self-judgments and insecurities leave. Now I am not talking about joining a religious group or church; I am talking about believing in a higher power and finding your divine self. It will open; all you have to do is connect by asking your angels for divine knowledge. It will open your mind to infinite possibilities, helping you move forward in this life to achieve your highest good, empowering and improving your quality of life.

All you have to do is call them in and tell them what you truly desire in and what you want in this life. You must be very specific in what you ask for because that is exactly what you are going to get.

Now you are manifesting your reality—your new life—and exactly what you desire.

Drop the self-doubt, and let the self-judgment go. They no longer belong to you because you were created to live your very best life. You are meant to fulfill your dreams. All it takes is letting go of your past, determination, and persistence. Just because you failed once does not mean you should quit. Keep moving forward. Let your life flow, then soon you will see your dreams and hopes start coming true. You are the master of your life. After all, it is your life and no one else's. Use the angels to help you throughout your life to help you gain the knowledge and understanding that self-judgment has been holding you back from the life you truly desire and deserve.

You have to learn to love yourself! That is the hardest thing for us to do. We love our families, we love our friends, but we can't seem to love ourselves. Why? Because you have been told by someone in your life that you are unlovable. Perhaps it was said in anger; there can be a thousand reasons as to why. However, trust me when I tell you no matter what has happened to you or what was said to you, you can overcome them. No one else can do this for you. You have to take control of your own life. You do not need permission from anyone. Let your imagination run free.

This allows you to open your heart and see that you are a work of art—God's greatest masterpiece—that you are not ordinary. It will let you see beyond others, introducing you to a world of love, grace, truth, and joy. You can love others, see within yourself, and privately explore yourself and your life in a new and positive way through God and the angels.

Don't limit yourself to a narrow spectrum because you have unlimited possibilities. Others have taught you to be judgmental of yourself, to listen to their words and that they are the wise ones when they are mere mortals, not knowing any more than you. By opening the door to your "God self," you can have a new and positive life of divine love. By letting go of self-doubt, you will have unlimited possibilities.

Metaphysical moment:

Are you aware?

10

AWARENESS

Awareness is the key to everything in this life. Are you aware of your "God self" and the spiritual side of your life? Awareness is the key to being happy, staying away from an issue that arises, including others and what they say, and thinking for ourselves.

When you meet someone, do they make you feel good, or do they make the hairs on the back of your neck stand up? Have you walked into a place and felt like you want to leave immediately? Does gut tell you to stay home when you are on your way out the door? Could it be that that feeling is helping to keep you out of danger someway—perhaps a car accident or a bad case of the flu from where you were going. When you get that gut feeling, pay attention to it. Listen! The gut and heart will always let you know what is good and what is bad.

I am a master Reiki practitioner, and I work with energy, so I not only have lots of healing energy that always surround me; I also can detect negative or bad energy. I am always aware of my surroundings, feeling the energy and listening to my gut! I have walked into a store and immediately walked out; I was not supposed to go there. There is a reason. I may not know the reason at that time, but whatever it was, I was not to go there. I may wait fifteen minutes and go back and everything feels fine. In other words, I get the green light.

You have to remember—this is your personal journey, no one else's. It may feel okay to the person you are with; however, if it gives you warning bells, do not do it. Awareness is the key to knowing what is right or wrong for you. Know your surroundings.

I am a seer, so I see the whole of things—people, cars, buildings, animals, etc. I look beyond the ordinary because the ordinary can change in a blink of the eye especially if you are alone when traveling or shopping.

Awareness is not fearing; it is a knowing and listening to your gut. I let God and the angels give me the messages and knowledge I need at that moment. When you learn how to use the angels, they make your day go so much easier. They truly lighten your day as they light the way for you to go.

Over the years, the angels have shown me that awareness is the key to living a life filled with promise, love, joy, and tranquility. Isn't that what we all are looking for? Why live a life of fear, anger, envy, and jealousy? These things are what is holding you back from truly living your life of freedom. Open your mind and heart to new and wonderful experiences. It truly is not that hard to do. God and the angels will help you in this life if you let them, not man or greed.

First, call your angels in; we all have them. Even if you have never used them, they are with you. I am blessed because I see angels; most people do not. Call them in your mind, and let them know that you need their help. We all need help in our daily lives. Then ask them to give you the gift of awareness, then sit quietly for a few minutes. You may not hear them, but you will notice how great your day has become. I use them for everything including writing this for you! They are truly miracle workers. You will start noticing more things, people, places in your life. It really eases your mind—from keeping you from overthinking a problem to manifesting what you want out of this life.

Are you aware of yourself and your actions? Most people are really not. Are you seen by others as an aggressive person? Are you seen as a very shy person? A confident person? Or you seen as a negative or a positive person?

In some cases, it is not how you perceive yourself but how others perceive you. We need to be consciously aware of how others perceive us, the reason being people only see one side of someone they don't know, and they can draw the wrong conclusion of them immediately. It happens all the time. I have met people who seem to be a genuinely nice person and later found out they are a completely different person with the heart of a venomous snake.

So we cannot judge someone else, and we also cannot change them; they are on their own path. We need to stay on our own path. We learn our lesson and move on. Trust your angels to give you the warning signs you need to be listening to.

Are you aware?

Metaphysical moment:

*Enjoy this heavenly earth and
universe filled with wonders
and miracles of the stars.
Most of all, stand on
your mountain, and
enjoy being you.*

11

WE ARE BOUNDLESS

We are boundless. We are the ones who set limits on our lives and what we can achieve! We set the boundaries. We have been programed to set boundaries when there really are no boundaries. We let others—mothers, fathers—man set boundaries for us. Well, cut those chains now, and learn how to fly and learn how to glide across waters, in your mind freeing you to achieve the ultimate life you want and deserve—no matter what age you are because age is just a number. Become a star in your own right because of who you truly want to be without any boundaries holding you back from being a happy, successful person.

As I said, we have been programmed since birth to set boundaries. Our families tell us to stay away from the trees; the grass will stain our clothes. The fire will burn us. The charcoal will blacken our hands. The rain will make us sick. So you get the drift of things.

Then as we get older, our bosses, mates—whoever—set boundaries *with threats*. You have to be at work fifteen minutes early to get ready for the workday. However, you are not paid for those fifteen minutes, but still, do you have to be there? We let this happen to us even though we are not paid; we fear being fired from our jobs, which we need to survive. Now we have people standing above us in a pulpit, making us feel small and telling us they are superior to us. We are to listen to what they say because they know. They set boundaries in our lives again through fear because if we do not do what they say, we are doomed—not only in this life but for all eternity—making us afraid of our actions, our lives! How silly we let others fill us with fear and set boundaries on us! These individuals feel, as they hold the golden chalice, that we cannot touch it because we are undeserving.

Well, let me tell you—God has never said that the person on the stage is any better than we are! He holds the golden chalice to intimidate others, to draw their attention to him! He says he talks to God and he is receiving this message for others. Well, guess what—we can all talk to God and his angels. We can all receive our own individual message from God, and every message for every one is different! Why, you ask? Because we are all different. See, we are all on our own paths. They are all different even if they seem to be like our friends, family, or neighbors. There is always a difference because we are all different.

So what I do is be different from someone who may do what I do. Remember that one of the biggest gifts we get are from God and his divine angels are the messengers and they will never limit you or set boundaries. Because we are limitless, we have no limits, we have no boundaries—only the ones that we ourselves set.

Boundaries are like shackles and chains, keeping us from moving forward and becoming who we truly want to be. They keep us from becoming successful humans in this life. The universe waits until our time is right and then unchains us and removes the shackles from us so we can truly have success in our lives, so we can find peace, joy, tranquility, and trust—trusting in ourselves through the Almighty and the angels. When we do, we have truly healed ourselves in so many ways. The more we let go, the stronger we become, and we find guidance, wisdom, and our divine missions and spiritual openings in our lives.

So it is your life; make it what you want it to be. Remember that you are the only one in complete charge of your life—no one else is.

Exceed the boundaries and limits people have put on you. Excel in your life. Be what is meant for you to be because you can be so much more than you are now. With your spiritual self, you can be so much more. So quit listening to others who do not know any more than you do. Open your heart, and listen to how boundless you truly are.

Metaphysical moment:

*Words spoken cannot
be taken back.*

12

POWER OF YOUR WORDS

Lies are like building a castle in the sand, never holding together, only to be washed away and exposed in the test of time. It seems in today's society that more and more lies are being told; then when others have learned the truth, the lies have destroyed and washed away, ending in nothing. When you lie to others, you also lie to yourself by convincing someone and telling them a story. A fairy tale, a lie, or false facts will eventually destroy their trust; you will lose a friendship or even love. Marriages crumble because of lies. Sometimes even jobs are lost because of lies. Too many lies are easily told but never forgotten by those whom they have hurt.

The trust they have had is broken; the respect others have for you is simply gone.

Lies are like predicting sunny weather that all of us enjoy; however, the lie blows the sun away, leaving a dark cloud hanging over everyone—the dread of a dreary day, a dreary life. The scale has been tilted, and there is no longer a balance in the relationship because of untrue works that were spoken and cannot be taken back.

The teller of the lie has just been run over by a huge bus! Usually when someone lies, they have something to hide, which they've buried deep within themselves. They are motivated by fear—the fear that telling the truth would mean they will have to stand up and deal with the consequences. They might even have to give an explanation or even have to say "I'm sorry." They have to accept responsibility for what they have said or done.

However, the truth is so much easier and a lot less distracting than telling lies. We are all human. We are sometimes wrong. We even make mistakes. We are even sometimes careless and break things. Sometimes accidents happen, so we tell the truth. We say

"I'm sorry," and we try to learn and avoid the wrongs in the future because what we do affects others. It is so much easier to build the truth on a solid foundation than to build a lie on sand by the water. It will certainly, and surely one day, wash away, leaving you with nothing but emptiness.

I have clients who think they are so clever that they can lie to me. *Wrong.* The angels see all and know all; the Spirit sees and knows all. The angels set off huge alarms when a client lies to me. Why? Because that person does not know the true meaning of truth! I have channeled and worked with several pathological liars. They live a polar life in a world of darkness, and they all are always suffering from severe anxiety problems, migraines—lying will take its toll on them after a while. Many relationships have been broken because they were built on lies, many a job lost because of lies.

When you lie, you are also stealing. You are stealing one of the most valuable things you can have with someone—trust. There are so many people who lie to themselves. This is the saddest one—the lie that says, "If I hide this or accept this and pretend it's okay, they think it'll be okay." These are the lies that will figuratively eat you alive because when you open yourself up and look inside and see the emptiness in your life, you then know the one you have hurt the most is yourself because you will never have peace or trust until you right the wrong you've created within yourself! How sad is that—that you've stopped yourself from moving forward in this life, that you've let a lie or lies become your life.

These lies you tell yourself are the most destructive lies you can believe. You are trapped in a world that you can no longer live in—a world that has destroyed your happiness and stole your joy from living the life you could have.

So it is never too late to reevaluate your life and change the outcome. It takes work; however, you can do it. You can have a loving and positive life.

Remember, your words have great power.

Metaphysical moment:

*When we grow, we unravel
our own self-discovery.*

13

Growth and Self-Discovery

Now is the time for people to open their minds and their hearts to all possibilities, to change their thinking, to open their world by doing what is necessary in life's truest form—listening to their inner selves, the God connection. You are never wrong doing this. The gut or the root chakra will speak out. The heart will speak out. The head will speak out in unison, bringing the answers through God and not man. We live for today, not for tomorrow or yesterday. Living in the moment of truth and when you experience even one moment of truth today, right now, you will change your life forever.

You will see that all things can change and the light will appear! If you only see the light for a few minutes today and feel the joy and peace it brings to you, then you will continue to search and touch the light tomorrow. What a wonderful gift God has given us here on this earth to reach beyond ourselves to God though a small space as large as the universe, though a speck of light!

This changes our course in life, giving us hope for the moment, the future, and carrying us to a higher plane, a higher concept, changing our thinking patterns, eliminating our fears of the unknown, making us individuals of time and space where there is not time, for time is a manmade illusion to control us.

Light is a spectrum of being, a guide to the inner self, to the other side of our thinking and being. Now we can truly know our God selves in human form. Everything then will start changing because the way we see things will then change, and the healing of oneself will begin! So things will lose their importance; others will start manifesting in a larger, more positive thing. So when you open the chakras and allow the thought process to change, your prayers are then answered, getting rid of fear and self-doubt, knowing the positive side of life!

Get rid of your "I can't," your negative side, allowing abundance of spiritual being in you to surround and protect yourself, giving you the knowledge and power you truly deserve, creating a powerful person connected to the earth and universe—as we all should be! Nothing is scary when the lights are on, allowing you to see. Only darkness holds the unseen, the fear!

By standing in the light of consciousness and surrounding yourself with it, you will create a new and different world. So, if for only a few moments, clear your mind, and focus on nothing by focusing on yourself and letting the thoughts, pictures, and colors come; you will be guided and told the answers. Do not fear the truth, but embrace it and celebrate the solution in you and your life. A change of the light force within you opens you to a realm of possibles!

Our lives can change our work status, bringing us more love and abundance. However, we have to love and accept who we are first. We have to be filled with the positive, letting go of the negative, charging our batteries, being human, and accepting God and his presence. The God source within us, whoever you think that might be, is knocking on your door. Please, won't you answer his call and open the door to expanding and prolonging your life, becoming joyful, happy, and at peace with all things on this earth?

Do we not see God in all shapes and sizes! We all come in all shapes and sizes.

Do we not strive in our own way to be perfect when in reality we are all perfect because God made us that way? When you take a wrong turn off the freeway, do you not take the twists and turns to get yourself back on the freeway? So why stay lost in life when all you have to do is turn around and go back to the freeway of life? Simple? Yes, the simplest thing you can do is accept who you are, who you can be, and find the God inside you! How? Remember to focus and listen to your inner you traveling through time and space, moving your life forward to a more positive and productive way of doing things—all done with the heart, mind, Spirit connection!

The preacher says, "Don't you want to be on the bus?" I say, "Hell no! I want to drive my own bus." You want to own, if nothing else, your life, your mind, and your heart; and with this, you are truly led to God in a spirit of consciousness and love.

The closest thing to "new" we will ever have is our bodies! Every day we regenerate—new blood, cells, skin, hair, nails, even new thoughts! We are new and whole every second of every day.

Metaphysical moment:

Forgiveness is a gift you
should also give yourself.

14

FORGIVENESS

For those who have wronged you, the hardest, healthiest thing you can do is forgive. Why? It heals the hurt, anger, and fear within you. You do not forgive the act, only the person who has harmed you. You will instantly feel relief; a great breath of cleansing escapes along with all the pain. You will refresh your life, releasing it, letting go of the anxiety that has tied you down like a weight.

Each and every time you do this, you become a healthier, happier person. By standing in the light of love, forgiveness becomes easier, so forgive those who have sinned against you; let go of them, and move forward on your path to a free and easier life.

Letting go of past life experiences is a very cleansing and healthy act. Example, if you were divorced or had an affair with a married man, these things could have happened years ago, but you still have stored things in the subconscious mind; so if you meet someone who may be the right mate, you are instantly kicked into the boat of swords, cutting this person totally off at the knees before you give them a chance. After all, weren't you hurt before? Weren't you wrong the last time?

That's why forgiveness is so important for your health and growth as a spirit in human form. We all have feelings; we all have hearts. Hearts mend! Forgiveness mends the heart, allowing a healthy flow from the heart to all those around you. God leads you to another door of life in this life where joy and love are your gifts. The choice is made, and the gifts have been received.

Metaphysical moment:

Let go of the path that does not serve you!

15

Different Paths in Our Lives

We are bound to others, past and present, by fear, belief, choice, and change.

In life, we search for peace. We try to balance and find tranquility. We all want to find love—love with someone who truly knows who we are and accepts us as we are. However, if you don't love yourself first, it's hard to find true and accepting love from someone else. So you change to fit their mold of love and what they expect from you. So you lose yourself, your value, and the worth of who you are. It feels so degrading; you feel boxed in, and you have lost you.

Some find it impossible to find the right love, yet for others, it seems very easy. You may ask, "So why not me?"

The first thing to remember is life and all things upon this earth are constantly changing! Here is what you need to understand. When one path ends, another one begins. Sometimes the rewards can take awhile; this depends one how you handle change. How many times have you tried jumping back on the old path because it feels comfortable—until you realize how uncomfortable it makes you again? You're not meant for the old path; it no longer serves your purpose in this life. You have to keep growing and moving forward in this life! You have to let go and accept change in a positive way. You have to go with the flow of things in your life. That change can be hard, scary, but also full of rewards in the end.

When you take the path given to you, it can be life-changing in a positive way. It allows you to grow and find strength in yourself; it allows you freedom of the mind. It is a knowing that this path will take you to new heights in your life, that true love worthy of who you are will find you. You don't have to hunt for it; it will find you because now you can see and feel your self-love and self-worth. You will look different, and you will definitely feel different because believing in yourself creates a new and wonderful confidence that you have never had. You are no longer weighted down by the rock of oppression but lifted up by your power. You and your angels have opened yourself to your God source, truly realizing that you are never alone but that you are a passionate human being looking inward instead of waiting for someone to tell you who you are and need to be, for you have become a self-aware person with love, respect, and confidence of your own being.

So be persistent in this life to obtain all that you seek. You are worthy and capable of having it all by accepting yourself.

Angels can appear in many ways! They help lead us home.

16

THE BUTTERFLY PEOPLE

Come, come, come fly away with me. The "butterfly people" are mostly seen by children. Children have so much love and kindness that when they see angels, they appear to them as butterfly people. The butterfly people come in and let them ride to their heavenly home on their wings.

Your next question is why butterflies? Where are the angels? Well, the butterfly people are angels. Angels can appear in many different forms and any form they choose. They appear and relate to people in a way that is not scary but accepted by the person or group of people, making them free of fear.

So why children more than adults? Children love colors, and that is usually what a child sees first as a baby. They love colors, so a baby will grasp a toy that has color before they will a plain white or black toy. They hold on to the ones with color because it has a calming effect on them and makes them happy. A child gets excited when they see butterflies. They will laugh and try to grab one when they are babies then as children get excited when they see butterflies. They will laugh and run after them. They know the butterflies will not hurt them. If there is more than one, they really get excited; but if you notice, they run after the bright-colored ones.

Parents buy children angel wings to wear for different occasions, and they run around, flapping their wings. Who taught them to do that? Sometimes a parent or teacher. Most of the time, no one has taught them. So how do they know how to use them? Some say because they have seen birds and butterflies that fly because they have wings. Now most children do not ask how they fly; they just know. They know if a wing gets pulled off that they are wounded and can't fly. Nobody told them, so how do they know? We have to remember that children are of God. They come to this earth knowing and having this knowledge. They just know.

Didn't you as a child run after butterflies and see one would land on your finger or hand and how happy it made you feel when one did? So when a child sees butterfly people and that child can hop on its wing and fly to heaven, imagine how happy they would be. Children are often more accepting of death than adults. They believe in God and the angels. They know in their own little way that in death, they will be carried home and be healed in spirit. So we should all bless the butterfly people that have come to carry a hurt or sick child home.

I hope this brings comfort and peace to the parents and families that have loved a child who had to leave this earth too soon. God bless the little children.

Metaphysical moment:

Don't forget to breathe. Now take a deep breath and exhale.

17

GREED, MONEY, FAMILY, LOVE

Some people chose money over love or any-thing else. They also become lonely when love disappears and all they have left is money. However, this still does not satisfy them.

Success does not always mean money. We can be extremely successful in our lives through love, though business, through goals that we set and succeed with and meet.

Some people choose money over love. When love disappears, they are so afraid to have someone in their life who might need some of their money. Then the miser sets in, and things start snowballing into fear—fear their money will disappear. The money miser pulls back and retreats from love and sometimes even family, but remember, they are only rich in a monetary way.

Then we have those who profit and stack their coffers from others. They don't care if the people they take from are poor! They only think of bigger cars, houses, trips, and trinkets! These are the ones who profit from deceiving others. However, they are really deceiving themselves. How? Because the universe always knows. God knows. You cannot buy your way into heaven.

What good is money without love, friends, and family? Isn't this a very lonely experience in this life? No real joy in their life. Do not get me wrong—we all need money to lie. We also need joy and love in our lives because without these, we have nothing! Too much money only brings you an illusion of happiness. Such moments are few and far between. If you are denying others, then you are denying God. You think you are stronger than anyone else. You think you can hide from God? Well, no matter the amount of money you have, God still sees you and your loneliness. In some way, he will open your eyes to your "God self." Then if you defy him, you are left to your own demise. Your money will then mold and dwindle, your mind will become dull, and you will become dimwitted. You will learn your lesson—the lesson of sharing and caring for others.

Money is great, but living your life through love and thankfulness and having compassion is far greater.

Metaphysical moment:

Everything changes in our lives every day!

18

Rapid Changes of the Earth

The earth is changing rapidly. The skies are falling. Floods and oceans are rising, flinging water everywhere. Wildfires are destroying our land and homes. Tornadoes are taking lives, homes, and living arrangements. We keep asking why. With one clean sweep of the wind, the dangers are here, and man is still unprepared, unaware of what lies ahead.

Instead of looking down to find earthly treasures, look up toward heaven and see the Spirit's light and love. You can no longer ride the fence; you can choose to die a horrible death with an eternal life. You were born with nothing and will leave this earth with nothing, but you will live eternally by

God's side. He is showing how horrible it can be; he is waiting to see if anyone is listening! Apparently, you are all listening to man and not God. Pray for others; pray for ourselves, listening to all that is happening, and ask God what he wants from you. Start by doing one thing at a time. It's like teaching a child to walk. Do small things first, and see where that leads you.

Many will commit suicide and take others' lives in the name of man. Terrorists are here among us, armed with swords, ready to strike. Let us stand together in the light, taking away their power. Do not fear them. Trick them into seeing that you stand unafraid with the Spirit, and the Spirit and the angelic realm will turn them away from you. They carry darkness in their souls and cannot stand in your light. Onward, Christian soldiers, stand firm on your path. Don't vary, for fear is what they draw more power from than anything. Show them that they are the ones who need to fear—not you!

Be the own creator of magic in your life. The more magic you see, the closer to God you become. The more you realize that others are no different than you, the more awareness you will receive. Do not be your own enemy. Do not walk around with unseeing eyes. Man cannot protect you from earth changes; only God can.

Do good, and give kindness to others. Help show them the way. Open your door to those in need. It not only helps them, but it will also help heal you. Always give thanks to our Creator, and watch your abundance flow.

Yes, we have earth changes, and we always will until the new earth of peace comes, so we must learn to put our faith in the Supreme Being, our creator of all things. We must learn to be aware of change because one thing is for sure—life is always changing, and so is the earth.

Metaphysical moment:

Let go of what does
not serve you!

19

RELEASE THE BEAST—STRESS!

Living life and connecting with others is one of the most complex and stressful daily ordeals in our lives. If we all lived on a mountaintop by ourselves with no other human contact, then we would free—probably not. There would still be survival instincts kicking in, and stress and fear would again sit on your shoulders, gripping you around your dainty little neck. So in order to release the beast of stress, see why we have stress, what triggers our stress, and why so many others are stressing us out!

First of all, there's the judgment boat. Have we not been judged all our lives? Have we not, no matter how hard we tried, judged others or ourselves? Let go of judgment! There is more to life than gossip and judging others.

Here's a little tip—we all are spirits in human form. We are all, at this time, *human*. We are all on our own paths—sometimes going smoothly; sometimes we're in the ditch of life. Everyone is on their own path. Go out and quest to find the life that fits you—maybe not a perfect life for all; however, all things in life are perfect and as they should be.

Get out of your pitiful pearl box, and remember that when someone overlooks you or doesn't include you, it may mean they are having a bad day or could have another purpose in mind. (1) You do not need other people to make you happy or sad. It's up to you to be happy. (2) Use your mind for a positive outlet and not a toilet bowl for dumping waste into your mind!

Look at both sides of a situation—at work, home, with friendships—see that more than one person is involved in all relationships! Someone somewhere is going to annoy you, and every few minutes someone or something else will, or it could be several in a row. So instead of giving in and ripping the phone out of the wall, stop, breathe in positive energy, exhale all the negative, and remember to tame the beast, for you are not releasing it. Let go of stress by remembering that angels fly, that there is a Supreme Being, and life is as wonderful as it will be tomorrow because life is what you make it. Learn to laugh, love, and dance, for there may not be a tomorrow!

www.ingramcontent.com/pod-product-compliance
Lightning Source LLC
Chambersburg PA
CBHW040729070726
47599CB00033B/1318